How They Lived in Old Settle

Pictures of Old Settle

(A New Edition)

Selected by
W R Mitchell

CASTLEBERG

Watch the birdie! Click! And yet another photograph has been taken. In this collection, the emphasis is upon people although you can only just pick out the driver of this traction engine hauling limestone to Giggleswick station.
Below – Who's for tennis? This court was at Marshfield.
Left – An outing to Castleberg.

Farm-bred geese massed in front of the
Shambles for the Goose Fair.

Illustrations

Front cover, top – General Booth, founder of the
Salvation Army, doffs his cap to the crowd in
Settle Market Place. The General arrived by car.
Left – Walter Bates, Pennine bus driver.
Below – Constitution Hill.
Back cover, top – Morris dancers in the Market
Place.
Bottom, right – Dr Lovegrove outside the surgery
of Dr C W Buck.

Page 1 – A day trip by new-fangled motor car.
Penyghent forms a backdrop.

Picture sources

The compiler expresses his thanks to those who
loaned photographs. The prints came from the
author's collection, also from Tom and May
Dugdale, Tom Faulkner collection, Giggleswick
School, Joan Greenbank, K and J Jelley,
Knighton Collection, J W Lambert & Sons,
Langcliffe Hall, Moss the Chemist, John
Robinson, Joyce Seggar, Derek Soames and
Harold Walker. The compiler hopes he has not
unwittingly used photographs belonging to
others. He made every effort to contact the
owners of individual pictures.

Typeset and printed by Lamberts Print & Design, Station Road, Settle, North Yorkshire, BD24 9AA.
Published by W R Mitchell, 18 Yealand Avenue, Giggleswick, Settle, North Yorkshire, BD24 0AY.

ISBN: 1 871064 29 5.

Settle Market Place in Victorian days, photographed by Dr C W Buck, whose surgery
was in the imposing three-storeyed building.

Foreword by
The Duke of Devonshire
(Lord of the Manor of Settle)

THE MANORS of Settle and Giggleswick came to my family at the time we acquired those of Bolton Abbey and Londesborough in the middle of the 18th century. Today, my Lordship of Settle is little more than a title, about which few of the people now living in the town will be aware.

I can no longer raise a private army nor insist on having a monopoly in the milling of local grain! My legal connection with the fairs of Settle ended in 1924 when the market place was transferred to the Parish Council.

Yet I still find pleasure in visiting Settle, and when travelling along the A65, I love to see the gleam of limestone scars beyond the huddled buildings of the little town.

It delighted me in 1949 to be invited by the old Settle Rural District Council to attend celebrations to mark the 700th anniversary of the granting of the market charter. Settle cherishes the memory of its past, as well it might.

Some aspects of that past, in the form of a collection of fascinating old photographs, are now brought together for our interest and pleasure. I heartily commend it.

5

An "umbrella" day in the Market Place.

A Remarkable Little Market Town

SETTLE, in North Ribblesdale, lies on the fault line between the limestone country and the millstone grit. It has sweet landscape and sour landscapes.

Settle straddles the old packhorse route between Kendal and the West Riding (a river ford is still known as Kendalman's) and, despite being by-passed in 1989, it still caters for a host of travellers and visitors.

An 18th century traveller, the poet Gray, compared Settle with a "shabby French town". Today, it is recognised as one of the finest surviving examples of an old Dales market town, having retained the majority of its old buildings. Well-separated by open country from other sizeable towns, Settle has developed a character and life of its own.

It lends its name to a famous railway, the Settle-Carlisle, which, threatened by closure,

was given a last-minute reprieve in 1989. The toot of a steam locomotive may still be heard in the town as yet another "steam special" goes by.

Photographs of Settle and its district taken by several generations of the Horner family are technically the best; this booklet features the work of other photographers, especially those interested in ordinary folk activity.

The Town Hall *(seen above)* was built on the site of a Tollbooth mentioned in a document of 1716. The present building was originally a market hall. It has been described as "Jacobean Gothic"!

The photograph of Blackie White *(on page 11)* was taken by J. Hunt. His subject lived in Constitution Hill and specialised in cleaning chimneys and whitewashing buildings, jobs undertaken in alternate weeks.

Upper Settle. The topmost photograph shows the Jubilee Tree, which still exists.

Swingboats on Castleberg

A reminder of the days when Castleberg was a Pleasure Park, with swings and refreshments available on the flattish ground at the bottom of the limestone knoll. Louise Kitchener was in charge for many years.

An old resident of Settle recalls: "Castleberg was run by the Kitchener family. It was popular on Good Friday. They charged a penny for admission! You could go on the swings and hobby-horses, but you had to push them! There was a see-saw. And you could buy pop or a cup of tea." An operational roundabout was to be found on Castleberg as late as the 1939-45 war.

The Runley footbridge, a metal construction that spanned the Ribble for many years until the construction of the by-pass led to the re-routing of the river.

Seen in the Market Place

Above – The creeper-covered building is now the NatWest bank. Adjacent to it is a former shop and studio of Horner, the photographer.

Right – Dickie Gornall, the miser, walking briskly across the Market Place. He lived at Studfold; he was reputed to have a substantial hoard of money, but none was found on his death. He was known to the writer William Riley, and is pictured in his book "A Village in Craven" (which deals with Stainforth).

Personalities of Old Settle

Above – The dapper John Whittingale Winskill, agent for Walter Morrison at the extensive Malham Tarn estate.

Left – Tant Rawlinson, tinsmith, who lived in Victoria Street, pauses to look in the window of the shop in Cheapside which has for many years been the property of the Lambert family. Notice the shell-form of the carved doorhead.

Top, left – Blackie White, who lived in a cottage on Constitution Hill. As aforementioned, he was so named because he alternated the cleaning of chimneys with white-washing.

Top, right – Betty Dawson (21 stone) keeps to the pavement in Duke Street.

Left – Dr. Shepherd poses in the middle of Duke Street; he was on his way to fish in the Ribble.

A Dancing Bear in the Market Place

Above – Settle Market Place, showing the "Naked Man Refreshment Rooms". As recently as the 1920s, the townsfolk were marvelling at the dancing skill of a (muzzled) brown bear. When the show was over, the owner led it towards Skipton.

Opposite, below – Geese from the farms of the district were driven into town for the Goose Fair. The birds had been walked through tar, then over chippings, to reinforce their webbed feet against the rigours of the journey to Settle.

Above – Vetting horses for the 1914-18 war; the picture was taken near the Midland Bank. Mr Vine, a Settle vet, was paid £100 annually for checking the horses. The payments continued until long after the war had ended. He wrote to the government department pointing out that his services were no longer needed. The reply was, in effect, that he should let the government be the judge of that. Payments came for a few more years.

A Lanquid Afternoon in the Garden of the "Ashfield"

IN VICTORIAN DAYS, the Falcon was a private house, not a hotel. It was owned by the Rev. Swale, who preferred to live at Ingfield Lodge and who let the big house to the Nicholson family.

The "Ashfield", large and elegant, catered for high society, in this case the Zion Garden Party, with the minister, the Rev. G.H. Brown somewhere in the crowd. The extensive grounds are now used as car parks. "Ashfield" itself is a social club.

Above – The Robinson family at Cragdale, Settle, in September, 1890. They had a tennis court which, in winter, held enough water for ice to form for skating.

Left – An advertisement for The Folly relates to the time when it was a good-class cafe and provided accommodation for tourists, who were assured that the beds were "well-aired". Tourists were doubtless more interested in tasting the pork and veal pies!

Right – Among the many local hotels was (and is) The Talbot, complete with livery stables. The advertisement (right) indicates that you could book your wedding and funeral at the same time. The orders would be quickly "executed"!

Above – A foal suckles a cow near the old Giggleswick railway station.
Below – The partly-completed chapel of Giggleswick School. This domed building, paid for by Walter Morrison, commemorated the diamond jubilee of Queen Victoria.

Right – Conversation piece at the head of Kirkgate. The shop belonged to Mr Shepherd, the grocer, and was later known as Shepherd and Walker, Chemist.

For years, Settle stocks *(below)* adorned the market place, from which they were removed by order of John Birkbeck, J.P. of Anley. They were taken to The Court House, to be eventually used in a jocular manner at a local carnival.

Working for the Railway

THE coming of the Turnpike Road to Settle in the 18th century transformed the appearance of the town as businesses were lined up alongside the new route. In the 19th century, the Midland Railway cut the town into two with its series of viaducts and embankments.

Above – E H Partridge, headmaster of Giggleswick School, unveils the name-plate of the locomotive "Giggleswick".

Left – Some of the unnamed men who over the years have maintained the permanent way of the Settle-Carlisle railway.

Right – The goods yard at Settle was extensive, with busy coal sidings. A goods shed was demolished in recent years. In the picture is a Midland Railway wagon and some machinery that was being delivered for use at King's Mill.

Above – Midland glory. A southbound express passes Aisgill signal box at the highest point of the line.

Right – The derailment of wagons of a goods train on a Settle viaduct. On the right of the group of schoolboys stands Harry Cox, who was to have a job with the Midland Company just before the 1914-18 war.

Above – Typical shunting locomotive used in the Ribblesdale quarries.
Below – Settle station. Notice the goods shed, signal box, sidings and water crane.

Their Country Needed Them

Two pages of photographs recall the early days of the 1914-18 war and the enthusiasm with which a large number of local men enlisted for the Army in a conflict that was not expected to last long.

Above – The cricket field at Settle was a good area at which to introduce some elemental drilling.

Left – Recruits who had marched to the railway station had a rapturous send-off by hundreds of townsfolk.

Below – Well-dressed, with cloth caps, even when camping.

James and Mary Ann Procter had a family of five. Two sons and a daughter, Herbert, Sydney and Doris, served in the War. When Sydney and Doris died, the family arranged for a stained glass window to be installed in Settle Church to their memory. Mrs Procter, as Divisional Lady Superintendent of the Settle Nursing Division (see figure in white, front row of ambulance picture) had encouraged her daughter to join up as a nurse. Mrs Procter died during the war. There remained Mr Procter, two spinster daughters and Herbert, a bachelor son. Notice the curious ambulance, formed of two tandems with a weatherproof stretcher in between.

Below – Rookies in camp. They regarded it as a "bit of a laugh". Before long, many of those who enrolled were to become far too familiar with the mud of trench warfare in France.

Show Business

Settle never had an auction mart, though livestock fairs took place in the shadow of the Shambles, which were originally used by butchers. The great agricultural event of the year was the North Ribblesdale Show, held in the area now occupied by the Middle School and soccer ground.

At a North Country Show.

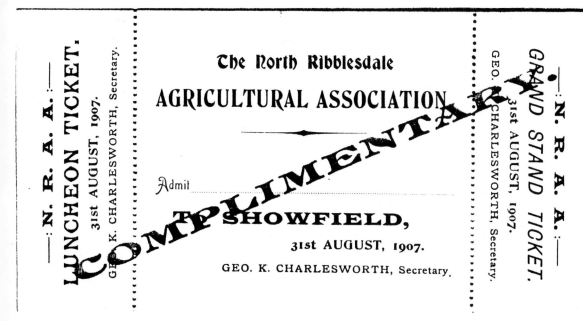

Settle, viewed from Giggleswick, before

nstruction of the Settle-Carlisle Railway

SEEN IN DUKE STREET (formerly Duck Street). *Above* – What is now Barclays Bank, with pre-war railings in front. *Below* – Laying the sewers.

Above – Building developments down The Gardens. Into being came High Hill Grove and Halstead Cottages.

Below – The Tanyard, from which – within living memory – came the nauseating smell of skins.

Below, right – A conversation piece in Duke Street, Settle.

Wesleyan Church
Settle

John Wills F.S.Sc Arch?
— DERBY —

Both Settle Parish Church and the Wesleyan Chapel, products of the 19th century, have turrets. It is almost as though they are standing on tiptoe, anxious to keep an eye on each other over the embankment of the Settle-Carlisle railway. (In fact, the Church was built before the line). Above is an "artist's impression" of the Wesleyan place of worship.

Catholic Church, Settle

The Terrace
Catholic Church, Settle.

The old Catholic Church (now a private residence). A new Church was built on land bought after the 1914-18 war by the legendary Father Tilman.
Left – The huge cross, with mirrors, which gleamed in the light of the setting sun. *Below* – The Church from its extensive grounds.

Catholic Church, Settle.

Above – Dr C W Buck and the operatic society orchestra, photographed in the Assembly Rooms, Kirkgate.
Below – His great friend, the composer Edward Elgar, stands in the rear of a group in the garden of the Wilkinson home at Hellifield. Elgar first visited the area in 1882.

Above – The Falcon.
Below – A house in Duke Street built by the quarry-owner John Delaney.

John Coates, of Rainscar Farm, was one of many farmers who regarded Settle as their market town.

J. HUNT

Hairdresser

And PERFUMER

Town Hall,

SETTLE

John Hunt (right) had his business premises in the Town Hall; his interests ranged from hairdressing to selling toys. He was also well-known as a jeweller, optician and dentist – in emergencies.

Above – A somewhat overloaded donkey cart off Kirkgate.

Below – End of an era: the motor vehicle takes over the Market Place.

Above – Victoria Street, leading to Upper Settle.

Below – Milk delivery by horse and cart. Driving the cart "down the Gardens" is Billy Shuttleworth, who lived in Upper Settle.

Opposite – Bella Hargreaves, shopping in Duke Street.

Above – A car bearing King George V passes along Duke Street.
Below – Church Street, in the days when lofty trees flanked the extensive garden of Whitefriars.

J. W. Lambert, a name long associated with printing at Settle, was a farmer's son who became apprenticed to printing at the age of 12 years nine days. In 1881, he started on his own account in a four-roomed cottage in Well Hill, then moved to Cheapside where the composing room and much of the machinery was on the upper floor (see pictures above and below, the bottom picture including the old gas engine and cooling tank; the beat of the engine could be felt in the shop, at ground level).

Opposite page, top – Another view of the Cheapside works, and a study of J W.

Below – Mr J W Lambert playing bowls at Settle with his daughter-in-law Sylvia.

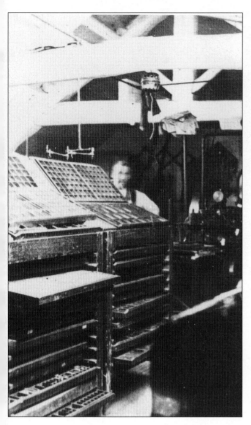

The High Mill at Langcliffe was one of the first cotton mills to be established in Yorkshire. The village provided much of the labour. It was augmented by workers from Settle, which lay within easy walking distance.

HORTON, LIME WORKS.

The once-immense quarry at Horton-in-Ribblesdale had sidings from which lime was transported over a wide area. A special goods train into Scotland was known as Limey.

HORTON LIME WORKS

Langcliffe quarry, adjacent to the Settle-Carlisle railway, had a large Hoffmann kiln with a central chimney. This labour-intensive kiln was for the continuous burning of lime.

Settle Market Place on the morning of the Total Eclipse of the sun, 1927. The eclipse occurred early. Soon the vast crowd and many vehicles had dispersed.

Royal Occasions

Below – The Market Place in 1935.

Above – The Jubilee of 1935 saw the premises of Kitchener Bros. festooned with flags.

Below – A celebration bonfire on High Hill. On the right is the celebrated Tot Lord.

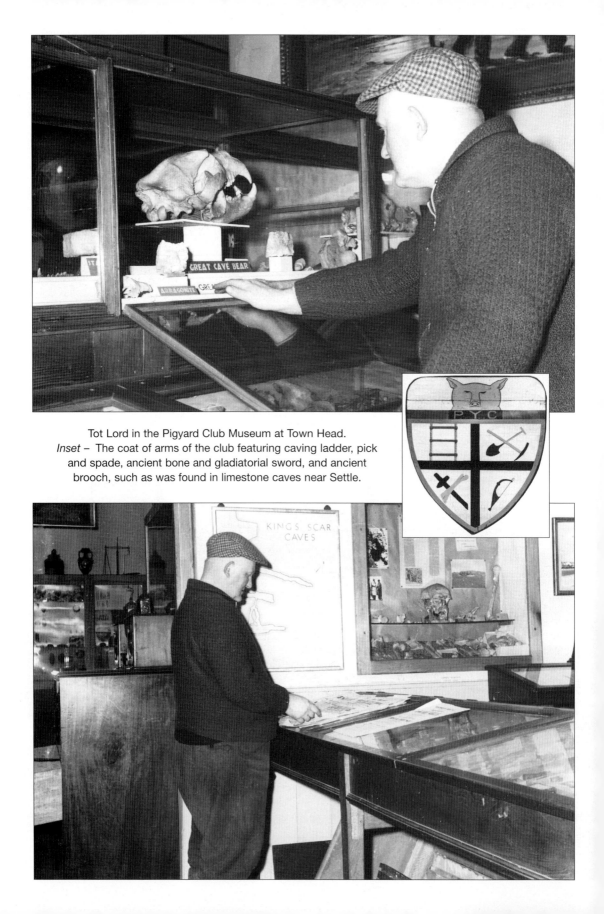

Tot Lord in the Pigyard Club Museum at Town Head.
Inset – The coat of arms of the club featuring caving ladder, pick
and spade, ancient bone and gladiatorial sword, and ancient
brooch, such as was found in limestone caves near Settle.

Above – Fair-time in Settle Market Place.

Cragdale, now a police station, was built towards the end of the 18th century by John Peart, a solicitor. The site had previously been occupied by a farmhouse. Peart was one of the first partners in the Craven Bank. The part of Cragdale illustrated *(right)* was for a time the Curlew Cafe. A story is told that when the farmer at Stockdale collected some sheep from Settle station and began to drive them to his farm, a number broke away and entered the cafe, causing consternation.

Above – An artist's impression of the great Snow Castle, built on the Green, Upper Settle, in 1886. Drawn by the mother of the artist Elisabeth Brockbank.

Left – Old Mick, the Bull Walloper. He is recalled as a man who wore a blue and white kytle (a lightweight coat of a type that appealed to country folk), also one gold ear ring. He is buried at Giggleswick, having requested that he might lie "under a tree where the birds always sing."

Above – Halsteads, the more imposing of many terraces built in Settle in the late 19th and early 20th centuries.
Below – A line-up of Settle postmen outside the Old Post Office in Duke Street.

Royal Wilts Smoked & Plain Bacon.

Finest Quality Irish Roll, Danish & Irish Bacon & Hams.

SLICED BY

Berkel's Patent Slicer

Every slice uniform thick-
ness—thick or thin.

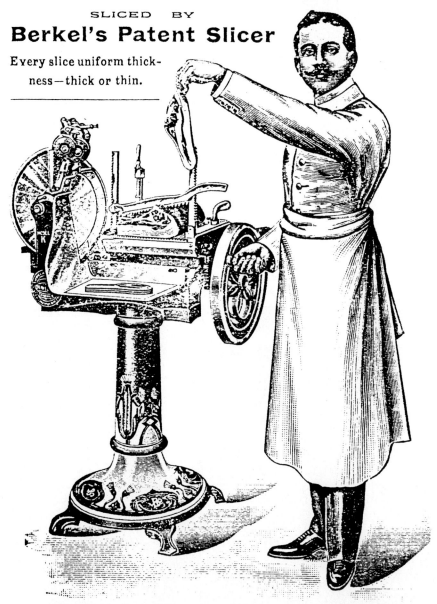

YORKSHIRE HAMS & BACON.

THOS. CLARK & SONS, SETTLE